Pleasing God

A Self-directed Bible Study for Living the Christian Life

Peggy Musgrove

Gospel Publishing House
Springfield, Missouri
02–0651

International Standard Book Number 0–88243–651–1
Printed in the United States of America

Table of Contents

Foreword

Every true believer wants to please God. In times of intense heart-searching this desire can lead to despair—if we look only within our imperfect selves. Conversely, when our hands are full of good deeds and our hearts grow cold for lack of communion with God, we may become as self-satisfied as the Pharisees of Jesus' day.

Actually, pleasing God involves a balance between *being* the kind of person He has called us to be and *doing* what He wants us to do. Peggy Musgrove beautifully demonstrates that balance in her own Christian walk. In this book she shares valuable insights that have come to her thus far on her journey toward "the mark for the prize of the high calling of God in Christ Jesus."

She takes what for many Christians is an ongoing question—How can I please God?—and explores the Scriptures for answers. It is as if she and the reader are studying together, discovering together how to apply the principles of God's Word to the Christian life and walk. In the workbook sections you can record your own discoveries and commitments.

Two things must be kept in focus when we consider how we may please God: (1) "Without faith it is impossible to please God" (Hebrews 11:6), and (2) "It is by grace you have been saved, through faith" (Ephesians 2:8).

This book is for those who are appropriating that saving faith and amazing grace day by day. May you grow both in faith and grace as you explore the attitudes, life-style, worship, and service that please our Heavenly Father.

ELVA J. HOOVER
FORMER SECRETARY OF THE NATIONAL
WOMEN'S MINISTRIES DEPARTMENT
ASSEMBLIES OF GOD

Introduction

How easily the words "I love you" tumble from our lips. We whisper them to our sweethearts; we mouth them in songs of love; we drop them casually to friends and relatives. Even in our devotion to God we sing songs of love or pray prayers that contain words of love and adoration. Like old coins, the words "I love you" can become worn from overuse unless we stop to examine their meaning.

What does it mean to say, "I love you"? Love has been defined as a concern for another's well-being, a desire to please the loved one. In one of those days that come to many marriages, I thought my husband had neglected something I wanted very much. Indulging in self-pity, I was thinking, *If he really loved me, he would be more concerned about what I want.*

My thoughts then turned to my confessed love of God. How often I have said, "I love you, Lord." Had anyone questioned that love, I would have been like Peter as he faced the cross and staunchly declared, "Even if I have to die with you, I will never disown you" (Matthew 26:35). Yet as I examined my thoughts, I wondered how perfect my love toward God was. If I loved Him truly, wouldn't I be desirous of always doing those things that please Him?

Those thoughts started me on a quest to know what pleases God. The goal of my life has always been to hear the words from the Lord, "Well done, good and faithful servant." This is what C. S. Lewis calls "the divine accolade." I reasoned like this: If someday I want to hear these words of approbation from God, don't I need to know what He approves of, what pleases Him?

Knowing God's nature to be just, I know He will not play games with us, making us guess what pleases Him. Surely His Word indicates the things He desires. As His follower, I believe my job is to discover what He wants and live my life accordingly. Consequently, I went to the eternal Word to discover what pleases God.

Pleasing God is designed to help you recognize the things that please God. To gain the most from this study, look up each Scripture reference and read it prayerfully, allowing the Holy Spirit to illuminate the Word to you.

Each chapter includes places to respond to what you are reading. Writing answers to questions and writing out Scripture verses will help you remember what you have learned.

You can use this study by yourself or in a group. If you are using this book for yourself, set aside a regular time and place in order to form the habit of Bible study. Read the Scriptures and meditate on them. Then record your answers.

For group use, appoint a moderator. Each person should complete the chapter before coming to the session. Have volunteers read the Scripture verses out loud. Allow time for discussion based on responses to the "Think About It" section. Answers that involve personal commitment may or may not be shared, according to your group. Conclude each session with prayer touching on the main points of the chapter.

1

The Pleasure of God

When we consider that God is all-powerful, has all knowledge, is unlimited by time and place, is the Creator of the universe, and sets up and takes down kings, we might wonder, *Does He not have everything His heart desires? Is there anything more that could give Him pleasure?*

Before we answer that, let us look at things God does not enjoy, things that do not bring pleasure to Him.

What Displeases God

Read the following Scripture references and list the things that God has no pleasure in.

Psalm 5:4 ______________________________

Psalm 51:16; Micah 6:7; Hebrews 10:6,8 ______________

____

____

Ecclesiastes 5:4 ______________________________

____

Ezekiel 33:11 ______________________________

Malachi 1:6–10 ______________________________

____

Hebrews 10:38 ______________________________

It must grieve the heart of God to look over the earth and see billions of people living in unbelief and wickedness. God did not create human beings to live selfishly or for sinful pleasure. It was not His desire that people would be cruel to one another, or greedy or lustful. Such a state of affairs brings God no pleasure.

At the same time, God is also displeased with meaningless religious practices performed in a perfunctory manner. Malachi describes people who were keeping the form of religion by offering sacrifices but their hearts were not in it. They were indifferent about bringing the best animals for offerings; they brought the diseased and injured. And even these were brought grudgingly. "What a burden!" was their comment (Malachi 1:13). Is it a wonder God was displeased?

What Pleases God

Though we do not worship by bringing animal sacrifices, we might ask ourselves some questions about our attitudes in worship and service. Do we offer God our best efforts, our best talents, our best time? Is our Christian service a delight or a burden? How we answer these questions may indicate the strength of our relationship with God.

When mankind displeased God, He could have abandoned them; they were not His only created beings. In the heavens are hosts of angels who always do His will, bringing Him pleasure.

Read Psalm 103:20–21. According to this passage, what do these beings do?

Nehemiah 9:6 tells us something else these angelic creatures do. What is it?

Like the angelic beings, human beings were created by the will of God (which is synonymous with the "pleasure" of God).

Read Revelation 4:11. What two things does this verse tell us about God?

___

___

According to this verse, God is not only the Creator, but He is also the sustainer of life. Without Him we would have nothing. Consequently, He must have a claim on us.

However, God gave us the marvelous ability to choose our course of action. We can honor His claim by worshiping and serving Him as do other created beings, or we can ignore His claim by refusing to do His will.

Those who choose God's will bring pleasure to Him. To confirm this, read Psalm 149:4. Who brings pleasure to God, according to this Scripture?

___

What is it about God's people that He takes pleasure or delights in, according to the following Scriptures?

1 Chronicles 29:17 ___

Psalm 147:10–11 ___

___

If we choose to serve God, this will affect the way we live. God wants people who live with uprightness and integrity. He also wants people who fear Him and trust in His mercy. To fear Him means to reverence Him, to respect His power and majesty. This reverential fear inspires trust in our hearts, for we know who He is and what He can do.

People who live in this manner bring pleasure to the heart of God. In answer to our earlier question of what could bring God pleasure, we discover that God wants the hearts of His children to turn to Him voluntarily in response to His love.

Gift-giving time for me is a challenge, particularly in finding gifts for my husband. He is one of those persons who has distinctive tastes. Before giving a gift to him, I am always asking myself, *Will he like it?* Another problem with giving him a gift is that he never really seems to need anything. He either buys what he needs for himself, or finds a way to do without whatever I think he might need, so that giving him anything else seems superfluous.

I also have a particular distaste for what I call "duty gifts," so I try to avoid giving him a gift just because the occasion calls for it. I always want to give him something that is a real expression of my love, the love that prompted me to commit to our marriage relationship in the first place. The greatest gift I can give him, however, is the continued commitment to that relationship. All other gifts are insignificant by comparison.

It is this kind of commitment to our relationship with God that will bring Him pleasure. In this chapter we have observed those things He does not like. We know that He has no real needs, for He is the Creator of all things. We see that angels are beings whose duty it is to do His will. What He wants from us is continued voluntary commitment to our relationship with Him as an expression of our love. This will bring Him pleasure.

How overwhelming and humbling to know that even though billions of people are on this earth, the great God of the universe desires something of us personally. He wants our lives and the love only we can give. If our love brings Him pleasure, how can we do less than give Him our entire being, especially when we consider who He is and what He has done for us?

To those who commit to Him, Jesus said, "Your Father has been pleased to give you the kingdom" (Luke 12:32). We become members of God's family and participants in His magnificent plan for this universe.

Think About It

Think about your personal relationship with God for a moment. Has your life to this point brought pleasure to His heart? If you have believed God's Word and committed your life to Him, He delights in you.

If you think your life has been displeasing to God, He also has made provision for you through Jesus Christ. As we confess our sins, those things that bring displeasure to God, He forgives us and cleanses us from all unrighteousness. (See 1 John 1:9.) Then we begin living our lives in a manner pleasing to Him.

When you say, "I love you, Lord," do you give those words meaning by following them with actions that express love? Are you living your life with the hope of hearing God say, "Well done, good and faithful servant"?

List two things you could do to strengthen your commitment.

____

____

Write a summary sentence to affirm your commitment to God.

____

____

____

Notes

2

Enoch's Walk with God

Is it possible to please God completely? Again, for answers we go to the Word of God. There we make the wonderful discovery that men and women have pleased God. If they can do it, we can too. We study their lives to see what we can learn.

Enoch, the seventh descendant from Adam, was such a man. Our first introduction to him is in Genesis 5:18–24. Read these verses and record what you learn about Enoch.

Most of what we are told about Enoch is ordinary. He was born, he lived, he fathered children. But the extraordinary is also mentioned: "Enoch walked with God" (Genesis 5:24). That made all the difference in his life. Because one day, in the course of Enoch's everyday living and walking with God, God "took him." He was translated into the presence of God, as was Elijah in later years (2 Kings 2:11). And both examples foreshadow the great catching away of believers who are alive at the coming of the Lord (1 Thessalonians 4:17).

A further detail about Enoch's life was recorded thousands of years later by the New Testament writer Jude. Read Jude 14 and 15 and summarize what you learn about Enoch.

The only other reference to Enoch in Scripture is in the great faith chapter of Hebrews, where he is listed with the heroes of faith. Read Hebrews 11:5. What does this tell us about Enoch's life before he was translated?

Enoch "pleased God," and this was all that mattered about his life. The word used here for "pleased" can be translated "to gratify entirely." James Moffatt in his translation of the New Testament says that Enoch "satisfied God" and adds this footnote," 'Satisfy' is used in the sense of a servant giving satisfaction to his master."

What qualities are necessary for a servant to completely satisfy his master? While overseas visiting missionaries who needed locals to help them make the adjustments to the new culture, I had occasion to make some observations about servants. What does one look for in good help? One missionary friend thought she had found just the boy to help with household chores. Then she discovered that he spoke only the national language, no English. Unfortunately, she did not speak the national language, so they could not communicate. Communication is vital to a satisfactory relationship.

Another time I needed help in making travel arrangements, seeing that my luggage was properly checked, passport appoved, and necessary forms filled out. These matters are time-consuming, and I was not sure I could get it done without missing my final meeting. My missionary friend assured me that his driver would handle it for me, that he was a man of absolute integrity. I realized that dependability and trustworthiness are essential for a satisfactory relationship.

I am a servant of God. For my service to be acceptable to Him, to satisfy Him, I must be able to communicate with Him. He speaks to me through His Word; I communicate with Him through prayer and meditation on His Word. I must also be a servant who is dependable and trusthworthy, faithfully doing God's will. Then I will be a servant who pleases Him.

Enoch was such a servant. In reviewing the Scriptures about Enoch's life we can make some summary statements about him.

Enoch's Fellowship with God

The concept of daily communion with God will become a chief theme of our studies. It is introduced here as an element of Enoch's life that pleased God. Why does this please Him?

For the answer, we go back to the Garden of Eden, the place of the first sin. Before their sin, Adam and Eve walked in communion with God. After their sin, this fellowship was lost. According to Genesis 3:8, what was their response to God after they had sinned?

____

God, the Holy One, cannot walk with a sinful people. Yet His heart desires fellowship and communion. He waits for anyone to walk in daily fellowship with Him.

Enoch responded, finding fellowship and communion with God.

Enoch's World

We might think it was easy for Enoch to walk with God, until we begin to understand his times. Even though he was only seven generations from Adam, Enoch lived in a very wicked society. He was the descendant of Adam's son, Seth, the forefather of the nation of Israel.

But the Scriptures also record the descendants of Adam's other son, Cain. Lamech, the seventh descendant of Adam in that family line, was a vengeful man who gloated over his excessive retaliation. We know that in just three generations after Enoch the people had become so corrupt that God destroyed them from the earth and started over with the family of Noah.

It was in this kind of society that Enoch "walked with God." He did not let the evil that surrounded him influence and control his life. As a matter of fact, according to Jude, God entrusted Enoch with a prophetic word (a word about God's coming judgment, which is yet to be fulfilled).

Enoch's Purity

Fellowship with God should affect the way we live. We can begin to view life through the eyes of a holy God. Fellowship with Him becomes so satisfying that we do not want to do anything that would break the relationship.

This relationship became the controlling factor of Enoch's life. He witnessed to those around him, warning them of coming judgment upon their ungodliness. If Enoch was prophesying in this way and if he walked with the Lord, we can assume that he was living a life of moral purity. For a person becomes like those he fellowships with. Enoch's closest fellowship was with a holy God. Such a relationship had to have a profound effect on his life.

Enoch's Faith

How was Enoch able to live a godly life while surrounded by such wickedness? How could he witness when no one was listening? The Book of Hebrews gives the answer. Enoch had a faith that pleased God.

Read Hebrews 11:6. Here we learn that it is impossible to please God without faith. Two elements of faith are given in the verse. Record these.

____

____

The faith that pleases God, first, believes in God's existence—simply that "He is." This is the foundation, the first step in living a life that pleases God. We must settle all doubts about the reality of God's existence.

Consider that the Bible itself makes no attempt to prove the existence of God. It begins simply, "In the beginning God . . ." It is a given, like that of a scientific experiment. For example, if you want to prove you can combine hydrogen and oxygen to make water in the formula H_2O, hydrogen and oxygen are givens. You do not have to prove that hydrogen and oxygen exist. All you are attempting to prove is that with the proper combination these gases will liquefy into water. In the same way, the Bible assumes the existence of God—it is a given—and goes on to show He is a God who loves lost humanity.

Do you believe there is a God? If you answer yes, you are a person who has at least some faith, and that pleases God.

However, simply believing in God's existence answers none of the questions about His nature. The second element of faith is a belief that not only does God exist, but that He also responds to those who seek Him. Some believe in a God who created the universe and abandoned it as a child would a broken toy. But the faith that pleases God does not view Him in this manner. Faith says I believe in God, and I believe He will respond to me when I call on Him. This is the kind of faith that pleases God very much.

Enoch's life teaches us that it is possible to please God. We please Him when we walk in daily fellowship with Him. We please Him when we live morally pure lives and encourage others to do so. We please Him when we reach out to Him in a faith that believes He will respond to us.

Think About It

Life today is much more complex than life in Enoch's generation. Countless demands are made on our time and energy. How do we incorporate a sincere walk with God into today's life-style?

Role models are important to us in the learning process. Enoch was a role model of a person who walked with God. Do you know people about whom you could say they walk with God? What is it about their lives that makes you say that?

List three things you think should be characteristic of a person who walks with God. Number them in order of importance.

____

____

____

Enoch preached to his generation about the coming judgment of God. The Church today is looking for the second coming of Christ. In what way does an understanding of coming judgment affect the way we live? What effect does the hope of the coming of the Lord have upon the believer according to 1 John 3:3?

___

We discovered two basic elements of faith in Hebrews 11:6, and that our faith is affected by what we believe about God. List some characteristics of God that you firmly believe in.

___

___

___

Based on what you have learned about Enoch's life, how could you make your life more pleasing to God? Write a paragraph below that affirms your determination to make such changes.

___

___

___

NOTES

3

Israel's Disobedience

Many generations after Enoch, God spoke to Abram in the land of the Chaldees, calling him to leave his own country. God promised Abram that he would become a great nation. Though Abram never saw the fulfillment of this promise, God kept His word to him. Giving him the new name of Abraham, "father of many," God—through Abraham's grandson, Israel—created a great nation through which He wanted to reveal himself.

The Bible tells us much about God's dealings with the nation of Israel, the suffering of the Israelites in Egypt, and the establishment of Israel in the land of Palestine through many miraculous workings of God. Knowing that these people were chosen by God, one might assume that to single them out in this way He must have been greatly pleased with them. But we discover the contrary, that He became very displeased with them.

God's Displeasure with a Complaining Nation

Read 1 Corinthians 10:1–11. What happened to the generation God was not pleased with?

According to verses 6 and 11, why do we need to study about them?

To find out what displeased God about that generation, let us refer to the Old Testament story. Read Numbers 10:33–36. This is a descriptive passage about the Israelites' journey through the wilderness.

How did the nation of Israel respond to this traveling according to Numbers 11:1?

___

The spirit of complaining brought the displeasure of God and the overthrow of a whole generation in the wilderness. What do we learn from their example?

___

___

For other New Testament warnings against grumbling and complaining about the way our life is going, read the following Scriptures. From each passage list one point you want to remember about complaining.

Philippians 2:14–15 ___

Jude 16 ___

Have you noticed that the spirit of complaining is contagious? Serve a group of children some food and let one complain about the taste. Before long all of them are shoving the food away.

Adults are not much different. Let someone walk into a room and complain about the cool temperature and before long everyone will be shivering.

A woman I once knew complained about everything. It was either too hot or too cold in the church. The music was either too loud or too soft. If youth activities were planned, she thought the elderly were being neglected. If no youth activities were planned, she thought the church was unconcerned. She cloaked her complaining spirit in terms of concern for the work of the Lord, saying she only wanted excellence. But her spirit permeated the congregation and hindered the growth of the church.

We should take seriously the injunctions in the New Testament against grumbling and complaining. The example of the judgment that came on the nation of Israel should be a sobering warning to the Church.

As we study the story of Israel, we might think God was rather hard on that generation to let them die in the wilderness. But we need to remember that God had given them two alternatives. If they walked with God, He promised to take care of them, to give them rain at the proper times, to give them peace in the land, and to put their enemies to flight. In addition, He would dwell with them and be their God (Leviticus 26:3–12). If they refused to follow His commandments, He warned that many sorrows would come. In spite of these warnings the Israelites disobeyed His word and suffered the consequences.

Read Leviticus 26:19. What was the core of the problem of that generation?

Pride kept the people from submitting to God's laws and walking in His ways. Even though God had provided for them miraculously, they thought they deserved better. They complained about the food, the route, and the leadership, all the while longing for the old life in Egypt. Evidently they had forgotten the hardships they had worked under when they were slaves.

Underlying the complaining spirit was hostility toward God. God told them, "If you remain hostile toward me and refuse to listen to me, I will multiply your afflictions seven times over, as your sins deserve" (Leviticus 26:21). It is possible for us to become angry with God when He does not act exactly in the way we think He should. If we examined our feelings we might discover that this anger has its roots in pride.

God made a provision for the Israelites, however, if they wanted to return to Him. There was a way out of their condition. Read Leviticus 26:40–42. What did these people have to do to be restored to a right relationship with God?

In every generation, God is willing to accept those who turn to Him in humility of heart. Confession of sin to Him and repentance are the keys to a restored relationship.

God's Displeasure with Disobedience

God's plan for the nation of Israel included plans for other nations. According to His Word that He revealed to Israel, through them He wanted to bring all nations to himself. But it did not happen that way. Not only did the first generation brought out of Egypt disobey God, but successive generations disobeyed as well.

Many years later the prophet Isaiah spoke to the nation of Israel, warning them of their sins and God's displeasure. Read Isaiah 59:1–15. Compile a description of these people.

Hands ______________________________

Lips ______________________________

Feet ______________________________

Thoughts ______________________________

Peace ______________________________

Justice ______________________________

Truth ______________________________

These people who had given themselves over to wickedness had lost the peace of God. Justice and truth were missing from their society. What was God's response to them?

____

God's Ultimate Relationship with Israel

The history of this nation is blotted with times of rebellion against God and failure to live according to the truth of His Word. For a brief summary of this history read Nehemiah 9:5–31.

In spite of Israel's many failures, God will ultimately be pleased with them. Many passages in Scripture point to the time when God will restore the nation to himself. The reason for this is that God is a covenant-keeping God. He will remember His covenant with Abraham. Even though the nation of Israel failed, God is true to His covenant (Nehemiah 9:32).

To what does God compare His future relationship with Israel, according to Isaiah 62:1–5?

____

The love relationship of a bridegroom with his bride is used as an illustration of how God feels toward Israel. His covenant is a covenant of love.

Think About It

According to 1 Corinthians 10:6, we are to take the history of Israel as an example. Spend some time meditating on what you have read to see how it applies to our generation.

Think about the grumbling and complaining generation that was lost in the wilderness. What similarities do you see to people today? List the first three that come to your mind.

____

____

____

Do you think complaining is sin? If we have fallen into the habit of complaining what should we do?

____

____

What positive trait should be substituted for a grumbling and complaining spirit?

____

Think now about the successive generations of the nation of Israel that also failed to keep God's Word and were disobedient to Him. List comparisons you see to the Church today.

___

___

___

We must always keep in focus that sin and disobedience displease God, who longs for us as a bridegroom longs for his bride. When we see Him in this capacity, our hearts should respond in tenderness and love. Our desire should be to avoid anything that might displease God, confessing sins that might grieve Him and thanking Him for all of His goodness.

When Israel returned to God in Nehemiah's time (Nehemiah 9 and 10), they listed those things they would do in obedience to God's law. In a similar manner, list one response you hope to make to this lesson.

___

___

Notes

4

Jesus' Example

The Old Testament ends with the history of a nation that displeased God. Even though Enoch and others did please Him, the majority of people chose not to. So we might continue to wonder how one goes about pleasing God and why it seems to be achieved by the few.

The New Testament opens with the beautiful accounts of the life of one person who stands above all other persons in biblical history. From the stories of events surrounding His birth, we know that this man, Jesus of Nazareth, is the Son of God.

Very little is told of His early childhood. On one occasion we see Him in the temple, amazing those He talks with. (See Luke 2:41–52.) What insight does this story give into Jesus' relationship with God and the purpose of His life?

____

____

Three of the gospel writers give us the account of Jesus' baptism, which was the beginning of His public ministry. Read the three accounts of this baptism in Matthew 3:13–17, Mark 1:9–11, and Luke 3:21–22. What does the voice from heaven say on this occasion?

____

____

This biblical account gives us insight into the loving heart of God, a heart that is illustrated by the love of a father for his son. I observed this fatherly love when I was at a church program featuring children. Over a hundred active children were on the platform singing for the congregation. None of the children were mine so I observed them all with casual interest. I had not even located the seven-year-old son of my friend sitting next to me, but I noticed the intense pride on the father's face, with a touch of a smile playing on his lips. He whispered to me, "Watch Jason's eyebrows."

I laughed to myself. I had not even found Jason, let alone noticed his eyebrows moving rhythmically with the music. But the father had eyes only for his son. Even the whimsical movement of his son's eyebrows gave him pleasure.

How much the Heavenly Father must have loved His Son, who walked in perfect obedience. His eyes had been on Him through the years of maturing. Now He watched as He began His public ministry. The love in His heart had to be expressed, so He spoke from heaven for all the world to hear: "You are my Son, whom I love; with you I am well pleased."

Isaiah's Prophecies of Jesus

From the beginning of Jesus' ministry we know the Heavenly Father was pleased with Jesus. Isaiah had prophesied that One would come who would please the Father greatly. Jesus was the fulfillment of that prophecy.

Compare Isaiah 42:1–4 and Matthew 12:15–21. Make notes from these passages of characteristics of Jesus that pleased the Father.

____

____

____

____

____

Isaiah pictured Jesus as one who would have the Spirit of God, who would proclaim justice to the world, and yet who would be meek and gentle. He would be compassionate and sympathetic, not breaking a "bruised reed" or snuffing out a "smoldering wick." Even in this gentle, nonviolent approach He ultimately would cause justice to triumph and all nations would hope in His name. With this man, Isaiah said, God would be well-pleased.

The Mount of Transfiguration

On one other occasion in Jesus' life God spoke from heaven. This was what is commonly called the transfiguration of Jesus, referring to the time when He was on the mountain with Peter, James, and John. Read the account in Matthew 17:1–8. What were the disciples told to do in verse 5?

Verse 5 ____

The Heavenly Father was pleased with His divine Son. God wanted His earthly children to listen to Jesus. He could tell us of our Heavenly Father, so we also could please Him.

Pleasing God was a way of life for Jesus. He was not concerned with doing His own will but with doing the will of the Father. Record the words of Jesus in John 8:29 that show this was His determination.

John 8:29 ____

____

Paul's Writings about Jesus

Paul's writings about Jesus agree with the prophecy of Isaiah and the accounts of the gospel writers. When encouraging the early Christians to be considerate of each other, Paul reminded them that Jesus did not please himself (Romans 15:1–3). Record the phrase that states this.

Romans 15:3 ____

The word Paul uses for "please" here is slightly different from the one used in the Gospels. The earlier writers used a word that implies approval. The word Paul uses involves the emotions and could be defined "to seek to be agreeable." It is as though he was saying that Jesus did not do what was necessarily agreeable to himself. He pleased the Father at all times.

Sometimes when we emphasize the gentleness of Jesus' nature and His submissiveness to the Father's will, we might not see the full picture of Jesus. Paul describes the supremacy of Jesus in Colossians 1:15–23. List five descriptive phrases about Jesus from this passage.

Verse 15 ____

Verse 15 ____

Verse 16 ____

Verse 17 ____

Verse 18 ____

In this passage we glimpse Jesus: His majesty, His power as Creator and sustainer of the universe, His deity, and His eternal existence. We see He is the Head of the Church, supreme in every way. When we see Jesus in this way, we are awed that He came in gentleness and submission.

God was aware of all of the dimensions of Jesus' personality when He said at Jesus' baptism, "You are my Son, whom I love; with you I am well pleased" (Luke 3:22), and on the Mount of Transfiguration, "This is my Son, whom I love. Listen to him!" (Mark 9:7). The Father knew of the Son's power and glory, and He was pleased at His willingness to come to the earth in the form of man.

This passage in Colossians tells a little more about why the Father was pleased with Jesus. Read Colossians 1:19–20. List two things about Jesus God was pleased with.

Verse 19 ____

Verse 20 ____

____

God was pleased that His entire being was dwelling in Jesus. Jesus was not "just a good man"; He was God. Yet Jesus was human, "tempted in every way just as we are—yet . . . without sin" (Hebrews 4:15). God was pleased that in Christ union and communion with mankind were made possible. Through Christ all things could be reconciled to God.

We must note it was not simply Jesus' living a good life that brought man back to God, although that was important. We have peace with God through the shedding of His blood on the Cross. His blood is the means of our reconciliation.

As we stand at the Cross, we comprehend in a measure how much God loves us and wants communion with us such as He had with Adam and Eve before the Fall. At the Cross we see Jesus, the perfect man who knew no sin, willing to take our sins so we could be reconciled to God.

Think About It

An old hymn contains the lines "To be like Jesus, all I ask is to be like Him." When we sing this hymn, we probably are thinking of His loving nature. In light of what we have just studied, list some characteristics of Jesus we should have if we want to be like Him.

____

____

____

____

____

From early childhood Jesus had a strong sense of purpose for being in the world: to do His Father's business. To state His purpose in another way, He was always doing what pleased the Father. Is it possible for us to have a similar sense of purpose in our lives? If we had such a sense of purpose, how would it affect the way we live? Would it affect the quality of our lives and our work? the stability of our lives? How about the spirit of competition with others?

Having studied this lesson, in what ways do you think your life is like Jesus' life?

What things could you change to become more like Him?

NOTES

5

Paul's Teaching

The ministry of the apostle Paul fills much of the New Testament. A major portion of the Book of Acts tells of his missionary journeys. Thirteen or fourteen of the epistles are Paul's writings, which many of the doctrines of the Church are based on. Paul too was concerned with pleasing God.

Paul's Call Pleased God

You probably remember Paul's story, how he persecuted the churches until the day God miraculously intervened and turned his life around (Acts 9:1–31). Paul knew his call came from God. Read his description of the call in Galatians 1:15–16.

How long did Paul say God had His hand on him?

Verse 15 ____

In what way did the call come to Paul?

Verse 15 ____

For what purpose did God reveal His Son to Paul?

Verse 16 ____

No matter what happened to Paul he kept this central purpose in mind—he had been called by God to preach the gospel. This knowledge affected the way Paul viewed himself. Read the salutations of several of his epistles. What three titles does he use to describe himself?

Romans 1:1 ____

1 Corinthians 1:1 ____________________

Philemon 1 ____________________

Paul's life was a series of dramatic changes. Sometimes he was a respected leader, acknowledged as an apostle. Sometimes he emphasized his servanthood. Even in a Roman prison he remembered his call.

Look back at the three verses and other salutations you may have read. In every case, whether servant, apostle, or prisoner, to whom does Paul say he belongs?

____

This tremendous sense of purpose stayed with Paul throughout his life. In one of his final epistles he uses three phrases to describe his ministry. Record them here.

2 Timothy 4:7 ____________________

____

____

Paul's Preaching Pleased God

Throughout Paul's ministry he maintained an awareness that he must please God. He would do this not only by submitting to the call of God, but by the manner in which he fulfilled his call. He was called to preach one message: Jesus Christ.

Paul was aware that in the ministry one was tempted to be a people-pleaser. What are some temptations listed in 1 Thessalonians 2:4–6?

Verse 5 ____________________

Verse 5 ____________________

Verse 6 ____________________

Instead of approaching people with flattering words to cover up a spirit of greed and self-seeking, Paul ministered in a manner that pleased God. To what did he compare his life-style in 1 Thessalonians 2:7,11?

Verse 7 ______________________________

Verse 11 ______________________________

Paul pleased God not only in his manner of preaching but also in the message he preached. Read 1 Corinthians 1:21–23.

What was Paul's message?

Verse 23 ______________________________

What was the world's response to this message?

Verse 23 ______________________________

What is this message to those who believe?

Verse 24 ______________________________

Again we are led to the Cross. In studying Jesus' life we learned man was reconciled to God through the Cross. This is the message that must be preached. To those who do not believe, this message seems like foolishness, but those who believe understand that in the Cross God's wisdom and power are shown.

What Paul's Life Teaches Us

We could look at a man like Paul and think, *But he was somebody special.* And that is true. He filled a significant place in the plan of God in the establishing of the Church. But he is not the only person through whom God wants to work. In Paul's closing statements about his life, he says the reward he will receive is not for himself only, but "also to all who have longed for his appearing" (2 Timothy 4:8). There is a reward for everyone who serves Christ.

Read Galatians 1:15–16 again. Here Paul states that the purpose of God was to "reveal his Son in me." This is also the purpose of God for every one of us. Read Romans 8:29. For what purpose are we called, according to this Scripture?

Verse 29 ____

____

God's desire for each of us is that we would be conformed to the image of His Son. To put it more simply, God wants every one of us to be like Jesus. This would please Him very much.

Throughout Paul's life he maintained this sense of purpose. He knew he had been called to preach the gospel to the Gentile nations. He did not swerve from this purpose for he knew he was pleasing God. He wanted to preach to the Gentiles so they also would become acceptable to God (Romans 15:16). In fact, he wanted everyone to whom he preached to be pleasing to God.

This sense of purpose came first to Paul at his conversion on the Damascus Road. What did he ask the Lord when he encountered Him that day?

Acts 9:6 ____

____

In telling about this experience later, Paul shares what the Lord spoke to him that day. Read Acts 26:13–20.

This is a question each of us must consider. What does the Lord want of me? Each of us must answer as God speaks to us personally.

It is interesting to observe that God rarely reveals His entire plan to us at one time. More often, He reveals only the next step. As I think over my life, I can see that this has been His pattern for me. When I first committed my life to Him, I knew it was His will for me to go to Bible college. At that time, I really did not know what would follow. There He led me into a relationship with the man I would marry, but we did not know what would come after that.

Step by step we have followed Him for forty years. First to one church, then to another. To district work, on missions trips, and in various kinds of of ministry. He has opened doors that we never dreamed of and could not have planned. His pattern is to reveal one step at a time, but He faithfully walks with us all of the way. Now in later years, like Paul, we are still asking, "Lord, what will you have us do?"

God confirmed the call to Paul through another disciple, Ananias. Read Acts 9:15–16. What did the Lord tell Ananias about Paul?

Verse 15 ______________________________

Verse 16 ______________________________

The rest of the Book of Acts tells how God confirmed the call on Paul's life by His providential leading. We can also expect this kind of confirmation upon our lives as God shows us what He wants us to do for Him.

Think About It

If Paul had been asked the question, "For what purpose were you born?" he would have answered, "To preach the gospel to the Gentiles." This is in a sense what he was saying in Galatians 1:15–16. If you were asked that question, how would you answer? Can you put your response in one phrase?

____

None of us is an apostle like Paul. Most of us will not even come close to the scope of his ministry. But each of us can have a sense of purpose, since "God does not show favoritism" (Acts 10:34). He needed one man to preach the gospel for the first time to the Gentiles. He also needs one person, you, to do what He wants with your life.

Paul not only considered the purpose of his life, he also looked to the end of his life. He saw a reward to righteous living which was not only for him, but for everyone who lives righteously.

Can you honestly say you are striving for that reward? What will that reward be? For an answer we can only speculate. It should be enough to hear the "divine accolade" we discussed at the beginning of our study: "Well done, good and faithful servant!" (Matthew 25:21). This is the reward for those who live in a manner pleasing to God.

Have you prayerfully asked with Paul, Lord, what will you have me to do?

This question will be answered by the Lord according to the talents He places within us, the circumstances we find ourselves in, the opportunities He places before us, and the providential manner in which He leads us. Our responsibility is to be sensitive to His Spirit and to His leading.

Write a summary statement of the purpose of your life at the present time, what you think would be an appropriate answer to the question, What will you have me to do?

NOTES

6

The Church's Goal

During Jesus' ministry He alluded only occasionally to the Church He would build after His return to His Father. The Church, which had its beginning on the Day of Pentecost, emerged as a result of the outpouring of the Holy Spirit. Many were saved, and the disciples were thrust into a ministry of teaching those who accepted Christ. The apostle Paul was raised up to take the gospel to the Gentiles also. This was the beginning of what we call the Church Age.

The Church is unique among social institutions. Every other organization is built on the commonality of the members. By that we mean people have something in common, so they form an organization that will further their goals. For example, people who graduate from the same college form alumni associations. People with the same vocations form labor unions. People with the same hobbies form clubs.

The Church, however, is a cross section of society. It encompasses people from all nations, all ages, all socioeconomic levels. The only thing people in the Church have in common is a faith in the Lord Jesus Christ and the Word of God. As Paul wrote in Galatians 3:28, the Church was a mixture of Jew and Greek, male and female, slave and free. Yet, such a diversity of people is held together by a common bond; they are "one in Christ Jesus."

The Church as a Body

One analogy the Bible uses to describe the Church is that of the human body. Read 1 Corinthians 12:12–27 where this comparison is made. The emphasis of this passage is that there are many parts but one body.

Make a list of comparisons that illustrates the ways the Church is like a body.

	Body	Church
Verse 12	____________	____________
Verse 12	____________	____________
Verse 22	____________	____________
Verse 25	____________	____________

God in His great wisdom created the human body, arranging all the parts according to His design. According to verse 18, how did He place the members in the body?

____

If God put together the human body, placing its members in certain places as He wanted them, does it not follow that the Church is also put together as He wants it? When I accept this fact, I am recognizing God's divine sovereignty.

Viewing the Church as a body will help us in several ways in our relationships. First, it will help us to accept the differences between us and others in the congregation. What are some comparisons Paul makes?

Verse 16 ______________________________________

Verse 21 ______________________________________

The eyes, the ears, the hands, the feet, are all needed in the body and yet they are very different from each other.

Second, it will help us accept our own place in the body of Christ. Just as I must develop an accepting attitude toward those who are different from me, I should realize that I have a significant place in the church body as well. I ought to believe God placed members in the body "just as he wanted them to be" (verse 18).

Third, it will help us in our relationships. Paul refers to three things to help us understand these relationships.

Verse 25 ____________________

Verse 26 ____________________

Verse 26 ____________________

Christian believers should care for one another. If one suffers, we all suffer. If one is honored, we are all happy, because of our unity in Christ.

The Church as a Building

Another figure used for the Church is that of a building. Read Ephesians 2:19–22. In this figure, who is the cornerstone?

____

Who are the foundation stones?

____

What is the purpose of the building?

____

The Church is not compared to just any building but to a temple as a dwelling place for God through the Holy Spirit. Paul uses the same comparison in another passage. Read 1 Corinthians 3:9–17. In this epistle he does not refer to the ministry of the apostles, but only to Jesus, the chief foundation stone. Paul does emphasize that believers are compared to the temple of God with the Spirit of God dwelling in them.

When I view myself as a temple of God, with the purpose of offering spiritual sacrifice, I have a tremendous sense of purpose. What does it matter if I am rich or poor, recognized or unrecognized? I can still offer spiritual sacrifices to God.

The human spirit may be housed in a fragile body but it can soar to God in a constant fragrance of worship. This understanding helped me as I visited a nursing home where a great man of God was confined to continual care. He could no longer communicate with friends and family. In the natural I questioned why. But then I remembered that only his body was weakened. Who knows what spiritual communion he experienced with God?

Remembering that I am a temple also keeps me from degenerating into being just an ordinary building—a building, perhaps, where merchandise trades hands. This becomes the sole purpose of many who trade their time for money and goods. People who have no spiritual dimension, who live only for pleasure or gain, are like buildings in a public square where daily transactions of buying and selling are made. Nothing in their lives lifts another soul up. But the person who lives as a temple of God's Spirit has a dimension that, like a church steeple, continually turns people's thoughts toward God.

Peter picks up the comparison of the Christian life to a temple in 1 Peter 2:5. As living stones, he says, we are built into a spiritual house.

What is the purpose of this spiritual house?

Just as a temple is built for the purpose of offering sacrifices in worship to God, the believer's purpose as a spiritual house is to offer spiritual sacrifices to God. We will discuss these sacrifices in chapter 7.

At this point, let us just note that this spiritual house with its spiritual sacrifices is "acceptable to God." The sense of this phrase is that God receives what we offer Him. Or, to put it in terms of our study, He is pleased with this kind of sacrifice.

The Church as a Bride

Another figure used to show the relationship of the Church and Christ is that of a bride and a bridegroom. When Paul was writing to the Corinthians and urging them with great earnestness to live holy lives, he made this comparison.

Read 2 Corinthians 11:2. What was Paul's desire for the believers he was writing to?

In Ephesians 5 Paul uses the relationship of Christ to the Church as an example of the relationship between a husband

and wife. Looking at Ephesians 5:25–27, list four things Christ did for the Church.

Verse 25 ______________________________

Verse 25 ______________________________

Verse 26 ______________________________

Verse 27 ______________________________

When we realize how much Jesus loves us—so much that He was willing to give His life for us to sanctify us so we could one day live with Him—our response should also be one of love. Our only desire should be to please Him.

Think About It

Consider the comparison of the Church to the human body. The body has many separate and distinct parts, yet all are connected into one. What does this teach us about the interrelationship of Christians?

Consider how nourishment flows throughout the body. In what way do Christians nurture each other?

Consider how carefully parts of the human body watch out for and coordinate with each other, for example, movements of the eyelid on behalf of the eyeball. Shouldn't the same care occur between members of the body of Christ?

If I believe that God is the designer of the Church, just as He is the Creator of my body, how should that affect the way I view people in the congregation? How should it affect the way I view positions in the church?

Think about your local church as a building and yourself as a stone. Are the implications the same as in the previous comparison? How are they the same? In what way are they different?

Not only is the Church collectively compared to a building, but individuals are also called the temple of God. When you see yourself as a home of the Holy Spirit, how does that affect the way you feel about yourself? How does it affect the way you live your life?

Just as God's relationship to the Israelites was based on His love, so is Christ's relationship to the Church. In our study of the history of Israel, we saw that as a nation the people displeased God, ignoring His love. Now we put ourselves in their place. If someone were writing our history, would he say we are pleasing or displeasing to Christ?

Write a sentence to summarize the way in which you, as a temple of the Holy Spirit, choose to please God.

____

____

Write another sentence to summarize the way in which you see that it has pleased God to place you in the building, His Church.

____

____

Notes

7

Pleasing God in Our Worship

Our studies thus far have been an introduction to the concept of pleasing God. We have looked at people and groups that have either pleased or displeased God. Having examined both the concept and the possibility of pleasing Him, we now look for concrete ways of achieving it.

One Scripture will be the basis for the next three chapters.

"Through Jesus, therefore, let us continually offer to God a sacrifice of praise—the fruit of lips that confess his name. And do not forget to do good and to share with others, for with such sacrifices God is pleased" (Hebrews 13:15–16).

This passage talks of praise, of doing good, and sharing with one another as sacrifices unto God. In this chapter we will look at our worship.

In our previous study we saw that the Church could be compared to the temple of the Lord. This comparison was made not only collectively, as a Church, but individually, as members. The believer's body is a "temple of the Holy Spirit." One purpose of a temple is as a place for the worship of God. If our bodies are temples, then one of our primary purposes is to worship God.

In the Old Testament temple, priests offered regular sacrifices while incense burned continuously on the altar. In addition to the annual sacrifices for sin on the Day of Atonement, there were voluntary sacrifices of thanksgiving throughout the year.

The need for blood sacrifices as a covering for sin was fulfilled in the death of Christ. He is the "Lamb of God, who takes away the sin of the world!" (John 1:29). Nothing we can do can add to His work for us. We simply accept by faith His offering of himself for our sins.

The sacrifice of thanksgiving was a different type of offering. It was presented not as a covering for sin but as a freewill offering in thanks to God for His goodness (Leviticus 22:29). Let us look at times this sacrifice was offered.

The Sacrifice of Praise in Times of Revival

During the revival under King Hezekiah, when the nation of Israel returned to the law of God, sacrifices of thanksgiving were offered. Read 2 Chronicles 29:20–36.

Which sacrifices were offered first?

Verses 21–25 ______________________________

What was the response after the sacrifices were offered?

Verses 26–30 ______________________________

Note that the sacrifice of thanksgiving was offered after the sacrifices for sin (verse 31). We must never assume that praise and worship to God cover our sins. Sin must be dealt with at the cross of Jesus Christ. When we realize what He has done for us and commit ourselves to Him, thereafter we respond with the sacrifice of praise.

Hezekiah's son Manasseh did not serve the Lord until late in his life. When he returned to God in repentance, he also repaired the altar of the Lord and offered sacrifices of thanksgiving (2 Chronicles 33:16).

The Sacrifice of Praise in Times of Need

In our study of the nation of Israel we learned that the Israelites did not always serve the Lord. Perhaps one of the darkest spiritual moments was in Jeremiah's time when the nation had been taken into captivity. Although it meant great suffering for Jeremiah, he remained faithful to the Lord during this period. On one occasion, while Jeremiah was confined in prison court, God spoke to his heart and promised him that one day the sacrifice of praise would again be offered in the house of the Lord.

Read Jeremiah 33:10–11. What happy voices would God hear in that day?

Another prophet, Jonah, found himself in a very difficult situation because of his own disobedience. His prayer arose to God from inside a fish, "the depths of the grave" (2:2). As Jonah remembered the temple worship, he vowed to the Lord an offering of thanksgiving (Jonah 2:9). We know that from these depths God heard and answered his prayer.

The Sacrifice of Praise and Obedience

We might ask ourselves, what good did it do to offer animal sacrifices? The answer is simple. Animal sacrifices were both an object lesson, teaching that atonement must be made for sin, and a test of obedience. But even in the Old Testament it was taught that God wanted more than the sheep and the goats as offerings. He wanted His people's obedience.

What sacrifices did God desire according to Psalm 51:16–17?

Isaiah also saw that God wanted more than animal sacrifice. What did he tell the people to do in Isaiah 1:11–17?

Two things are better than the sacrifice of bulls and lambs, according to the Old Testament. What are they?

1 Samuel 15:22–23 __________

Psalm 69:30–31 __________

The sacrifice of praise is more pleasing to God than the sacrifice of animals. But praise can never be substituted for obedience. The two must accompany each other. Read Hebrews 13:15–16 again and note that the sacrifice of praise must come from our relationship with Jesus Christ. "Through Jesus" we offer the sacrifice of praise continually.

How wonderful it is to attend a church that truly worships God! I find that the fragrance of a worship service can remain with me throughout the week. But I am also aware of the possibility of being caught up in lively worship without understanding that true worship must be accompanied by commitment to Christian principles. This occurred to me when I visited a church and asked about a woman that I missed seeing.

"Oh, she no longer comes here," was the reply. I was told that she had quit coming when the discovery was made that she had been having an extra-marital affair for several years. Through all that time, she had been regularly worshiping in the services as though she had no problem.

How could this be? I asked myself. I looked again at Hebrews 13:15–16; it clearly says that the sacrifice of praise must come from a relationship with Jesus Christ. Worship that does not flow out of this relationship is only a meaningless form.

We need to understand the depth of truly offering spiritual sacrifices to God and examine ourselves for any rebellion that causes us to live a life inconsistent with the Christian lifestyle. Then we will be free to worship God in spirit and in truth.

The Offering of Incense on the Altar

In the temple not only were animal sacrifices offered but also the priests tended the altar of incense daily, to keep it burning before the presence of the Lord. Of what is incense a type according to Revelation 5:8?

____

Not only our praise but also our petitions are pleasing to God. Paul told Timothy that to offer this kind of prayer was "good and pleases God our Savior" (1 Timothy 2:3). So for purposes of our study, we can add the prayer of petition as pleasing God. In fact, it is His delight (Proverbs 15:8).

For whom should we pray according to 1 Timothy 2:1–4?

Verse 1 ______________________________

Verse 2 ______________________________

Verse 4 ______________________________

According to 1 John 3:20–24, our prayer life is affected by the way we live. What commandments are we to keep to please God?

Verse 23 ______________________________

____

When we live with the determination to please God, our prayer life is strengthened. We present our petitions in the confidence that God hears us and will answer our prayer.

Think About It

The sacrifice of thanksgiving was not a mandatory sacrifice. It was offered according to a person's own freewill. It was offered in gratitude to God both for what He had done and in recognition of who He is. List one thing in each of these two areas for which you could be praising the Lord for today.

____

____

Frequently we sing of offering sacrifices of praise as we come together. And our meetings in which we praise God with singing and prayer we call worship services. From our studies, however, we have learned that sacrifice for sin must be made before worship is meaningful. Has your sacrifice of thanksgiving been made acceptable to God by your acceptance of the work of Jesus Christ as a covering for your sin? If so, offer thanksgiving for this also. If not, you can accept Jesus Christ right now by inviting Him into your life, asking forgiveness for your sins.

When atonement for sin has been made, and sacrifices of thanksgiving offered, petition to the Lord can be made. What petitions are you making to the Lord today, presenting them to the Lord as burning incense? Record them here.

____

____

____

Remember that incense was offered daily. Continue in prayer, praise, and petition until you know God's will concerning the matters you bring to Him. He does answer prayer.

The sacrifice of praise is offered not only in places of public gathering. Our theme verse says we should offer this sacrifice "continually" (Hebrews 13:15; see also 1 Thessalonians 5:17). So as you go about your daily work, offer to God "the fruit of lips that confess his name."

NOTES

8

Pleasing God in Our Personal Lives

Hebrews 13:15–16 follows the reference to the sacrifice of praise with the injunction "to do good." The implication is that our actions must be part of the sacrifice we offer to God. Again, we must remember this is not for our salvation. We do not "do good" to earn our way to heaven. Jesus has already made the way for us through the offering of His blood. Our doing good is an expression of gratitude to God for all He has done for us.

The phrase "to do good" can be defined as "beneficent action"; that is, action that brings benefit to others and to ourselves. The word "good" in this phrase is also the same word in the divine accolade, "Well done, thou good and faithful servant." If we want to be called a good servant at the end of our lives, we must be doing good while we are living.

"Doing Good" Defined in the Early Church

When the first church council was considering what requirements should be made of Gentiles who were accepting the gospel, they drew up a brief list and concluded it by saying, "You will do well to avoid these things." Read Acts 15:28–29. What requirements were placed upon the Gentiles?

____

____

____

When compared to the many requirements of the law, this list seemed short and easy. Nevertheless, the implication remains that what one believes should affect how one lives.

Living to Please God

Paul picked up this theme of living to please God as he wrote to the churches he founded. He emphasized their conduct should be acceptable to God.

To the Colossian church Paul wrote he was praying always that they "might live a life worthy of the Lord and may please him in every way: bearing fruit in every good work" (Colossians 1:10).

In writing to the Thessalonian church Paul enlarged upon this thought, listing what he wanted them to do. Read 1 Thessalonians 4:1–12. What things did Paul list as being part of a life-style that pleased God?

Verse 3 ____

Verse 9 ____

Verse 11 ____

Verse 11 ____

Verse 11 ____

Verse 12 ____

Paul repeats the charge to live free from sexual impurity. Immoral influences abounded then even as now. Paul reinforced the teaching that believers were to keep themselves morally pure, whatever their surroundings.

The other things Paul refers to should be an outgrowth of a believer's relationship with God. Believers who love God should love each other, living lives of quietness and honesty so unbelievers would see a difference in their lives.

Living in Light and Love

In writing to the church at Ephesus, Paul gives similar

instructions. Read Ephesians 5:1–10. What elements of a Christian's life-style are listed in this passage?

Verse 2 ______________________________

Verse 3 ______________________________

Verse 3 ______________________________

Verse 4 ______________________________

Verse 4 ______________________________

Now compare the two passages. What does Paul list in both places? What does he list only in one place or the other?

The repetition to be sexually pure implies the importance of this issue. Believers are constantly faced with temptations in this area and must always be on guard. To the Ephesians Paul adds the warning against impure talk and coarse jesting. His reference is to obscenities, what we would call the dirty joke or comments having a double meaning. He was not referring to wholesome laughter and fun, which is a vital part of Christian fellowship.

Paul also mentions to the Ephesians the need for giving thanks. This is a repetition of our study in chapter 6, but it shows thanksgiving and "thanks-living" must go hand in hand.

Piety at Home

Paul gave one further charge when he wrote to Timothy, his son in the gospel. He encouraged Timothy to teach believers to care for the members of their own families as an expression of their Christian faith. Read 1 Timothy 5:1–4. At the time of this writing many believers were widows. Decisions had to be made by leaders about provision for them.

According to verse 4, where does piety begin?

____

What does this kind of piety do?

How does God view these actions?

Paul encouraged family members to practice pious acts first at home by loving care of parents and grandparents. This is not to imply that believers should never seek professional care for the elderly, which is sometimes necessary. This, too, can express the care and concern of family members. The emphasis is that we not neglect family members, which is displeasing to God.

This Scripture passage became very meaningful to me at a time in my life when it seemed that caring for family was about all I was getting done. Two daughters in elementary school demanded much of my time, as children this age do. At the same time, my husband's elderly parents required a lot of our attention. I remember feeling caught between the generations, wondering when I would ever find time for myself and the pursuit of the ministry I felt God had placed in my heart.

That was when I discovered this verse in 1 Timothy that says God is pleased when we show piety at home. The care of family members expresses the care that God has for us. The family is the smallest cell of society. If Christianity can be applied in the home, and be made to really work, then it can spread throughout the social structure. If it fails at home, it will be powerless elsewhere.

This knowledge helped me to stay with the sometimes tedious tasks of daily living, knowing that my family was my ministry. Today, I have found time for myself and I am grateful to the Lord for the lesson He taught me early about the value of caring for family.

Examples of Beneficent Action

Paul wrote to the Philippian church while he was in a Roman prison. His circumstances were very difficult, so the Philippians sent Epaphroditus with gifts for Paul, probably things needed for basic human existence. Paul was very touched by this action.

To what did Paul compare their giving in Philippians 4:18?

____

How did God look upon their actions?

____

When Paul wrote to the church in Rome he encouraged them to go beyond sacrificial action and present their bodies as living sacrifices unto the Lord. This may be a familiar passage to you, but read it again in Romans 12:1–3. Paul wants the Roman church to understand God is not nearly as concerned about meats and sacrificial offerings as He is about lives that are offered to Him.

Read Romans 14:16–18, which tells us that the kingdom of God is not "a matter of eating and drinking." What three things is the kingdom of God a matter of?

____

If we want to please God with our lives, these three things will characterize the way we live. We will endeavor to live righteously, which is to be in right standing with God and man. This will produce an internal peace and joy, which are characteristics of the Kingdom.

Think About It

In the epistles to the Ephesians and the Thessalonians, Paul encourages the believers to live a life of love. If we were to receive a similar letter from him today, in what ways do you think he would ask us to express that love for fellow believers? List three things that come to mind.

____

____

____

Both letters charge the believers to live free from sexual immorality. Do moral standards for believers change from culture to culture? What can the Church do today to help people maintain a high moral standard?

Paul added that obscene talk and thoughts were also to be avoided. If we want to be obedient to this charge, how will it affect our living? our conversation? the type of entertainment we choose? List some choices that people need to make to keep their thoughts and conversation pure.

____

____

____

To the Ephesians Paul added a reminder to avoid greed, or covetousness. What are the marks of greed? What one suggestion would you make to control greediness?

____

____

____

Pious actions need to be shown first among family members, according to Paul's letter to Timothy. How can we teach our children to be respectful of elders? What can we do to show our love for the aging? Does this apply only to our own family or to the entire church community?

According to the letter to the Romans, the characteristics of believers should be righteousness, peace, and joy. How can we live in peace in a world full of conflict? What source of peace and joy is available to the believer?

List below any personal adjustments you want to make in your life to be pleasing to God, and to live in peace and joy.

____

____

NOTES

9

Pleasing God in Our Relationships

In the last two chapters we have discussed pleasing God in our worship and in our personal lives. The third thing that pleases God in our theme passage of Hebrews 13:15–16 is "to share with others." This is a translation of the Greek word *koinonia,* translated "communion" and "distribution" in the King James Version and "sharing" in most contemporary versions. A variation of the word is used in Acts 2:44 in reference to believers having "all things in common" *(New American Standard Bible).*

God is pleased when Christians come together in a unity of fellowship and relationship. This *koinonia* can happen when two Christian friends meet together or when thousands join for worship and celebration. The number is not important. What matters is that Christians experience the mutuality of their relationship that causes them to want to share their faith, their goods, and their fellowship. Let us explore some of the uses of this word in Scripture for better understanding.

The Sharing of Faith

In his letter to Philemon, Paul referred to the sharing of the Christian faith. Read Philemon 4 through 6. Paul's prayer for Philemon is that the "communication" (KJV) of his faith might be effective.

The most valuable possession Christians have is their faith in the Lord Jesus Christ. This we want to communicate, or share, with others. When faith is shared, a bonding begins that becomes as strong as family relationships.

How did Paul view his relationship with Onesimus, the slave he was writing about to Philemon?

Verse 10 ____

How did Paul want Philemon to view Onesimus?

Verse 16 ____________________

The references in Scripture to the "family of God" are more than figures of speech. When faith is shared, new relationships are begun in the family of God. This explains what happens when Christians come together, why we enjoy being with other Christians even though we may be very different from them in many ways. The sharing of our faith has brought us into a common relationship.

Paul was praying for Philemon that he would become more effective in this sharing of his faith. This prayer could also apply to us. This is part of what is meant by the reminder in our theme verse "to communicate," the communication which pleases God.

The Sharing of Goods

In writing his second letter to the Corinthians, Paul uses the word *koinonia* in reference to the sharing of material goods, specifically in the giving of offerings to the needy saints (2 Corinthians 8:4).

Read 2 Corinthians 9:1–15. Paul is sending a group led by Titus to Corinth to collect contributions for the church at Jerusalem. He tells them he has been boasting about their generosity to the Macedonians. Paul now wants them to gather an offering before he comes.

Paul taught them principles of Christian giving that can help us. His first lesson was from nature. What lesson is to be learned from sowing and reaping that applies to Christian giving?

Verse 6 ____________________

To reap a good harvest much seed must be sown. Paul wanted the Corinthians to have a rich spiritual harvest by giving a generous gift to the Macedonians.

How were the Corinthians to determine how much to give?

Verse 7 ____

Giving is relative to how much one has. Jesus' comments about the widow's mite (Mark 12:43–44) let us know that. And Jesus encouraged generosity (Luke 6:38), but not at the expense of one's attitude. What attitude were the Corinthians to avoid in their giving?

Verse 7 ____

What attitude does God love to see as Christians give?

Verse 7 ____

When the Corinthians gave cheerfully, they would learn "God is able to make all grace abound to you, so that in all things at all times, having all that you need, you will abound in every good work" (2 Corinthians 9:8).

Not only would they learn of the grace of God, but also believers elsewhere would give thanks for their *koinonia,* their "liberal distribution," to them (verse 13, KJV).

The Christian faith cannot be separated from benevolent action. We share our faith first and establish relationships with other believers. We follow with the sharing of our material goods with other needy believers. This practice results in blessing to giver and receiver alike.

The Sharing of Fellowship

Notice that it was the act of giving, not what was given, that was important in the gifts from the Corinthians. The gifts are an expression of commitment to the fellowship of believers. Another demonstration of this relationship is in Acts 2:42–47. What four things did the Christians devote themselves to after the Day of Pentecost?

____

____

The word used here for "fellowship" is *koinonia,* the same word we have been studying. A variant of the word is in verse 44, where it refers to the believers having "all things in common" (NASB). Christian fellowship and the sharing of material goods are closely related.

As we study this passage we need to understand what was happening. At first glance it would seem the early believers sold all possessions and formed some sort of communal life. However, as we look again we see that private homes were maintained (verse 46), which continues throughout the New Testament. The selling of excess possessions to distribute to the need of other believers demonstrated the intense love they had for one another and that relationships were more important than possessions.

When we understand the value of fellowship, we will do everything we can to protect the relationships we have with other believers. An older minister cautioned my husband and me in our early days of ministry: "Guard the fellowship you have with other Christ1ans." He wanted us to appreciate the value of fellowship.

The most valuable material possessions I have in my home are two antique porcelain figurines of the Bible characters Rebecca and Ruth. For several years after I purchased them I had them sitting out on the piano. We carefully dusted them when it was cleaning time. My daughters would warn me, "Mother, you need to get a curio cabinet for those figurines. If they get broken, they cannot be replaced." Finally I took their advice and purchased a cabinet. Why? I knew the value of the figurines, and I wanted to protect them.

These figurines are only material and will one day "be dissolved," as Peter tells us (2 Peter 3:11, KJV). But the Christian relationships I have with family and friends will be eternal. I must carefully guard those relationships from being broken, even more carefully than I guard my figurines.

Another older minister pointed out to us in our youthful ministry that people are usually very careful not to harm the body of another person, but many times will thoughtlessly do things that hurt the spirit. "Strange," he said, "for bodies will heal, but sometimes spirits never do." He too knew the value of Christian fellowship.

This fellowship of believers is an outgrowth of our relationship with the triune God. The apostle John wrote in his first epistle that he wanted believers to share a fellowship he had experienced. Read 1 John 1:3. What fellowship was John sharing?

___

Paul also writes of this fellowship. Read 1 Corinthians 1:9. To what are we called?

___

The fellowship is not only with the Father and the Son. Read Philippians 2:1. What other person is included?

___

Unbroken fellowship with God depends on our living in the light "as he is in the light" (1 John 1:7). Our fellowship with the triune God is made possible by the work of Christ. Then comes the hard part (hard because of our bent toward carnality and the influence of evil in the world), maintaining fellowship with others. But with this fellowship, this communication, this *koinonia,* God is pleased (Hebrews 13:15–16).

Think About It

The sharing of the faith is one of the first duties of the Christian. It is a fulfillment of the Great Commission left by Jesus. In what ways can we best communicate our faith? List ways you are involved in this kind of communication.

___

___

___

What should be the scope of our sharing of the faith? What are our obligations to our family, our neighbors, our community, our nation, our world? List ways you would like to become more active in sharing the faith in each of these areas.

Family ______________________________

Neighbors ______________________________

Nation ______________________________

World ______________________________

God's fellowship with us includes the provision for our needs according to Matthew 6:33 and Philippians 4:19. Our fellowship with others includes the sharing of our material goods when the need arises. How relevant to your church is the example of selling excess possessions for distribution to the needy? What is the present scope of this sharing by your church (considering the same areas listed above)?

Family ______________________________

Neighbors ______________________________

Nation ______________________________

World ______________________________

Unbroken fellowship with God is our highest goal. Our lesson series focuses on pleasing God. What principles have you learned from this study that will strengthen your own relationship with God? Record them here.

____

____

____

Notes

10

Serving God Acceptably

Our studies have shown us it is possible to please God. We have studied ways of pleasing God through our worship, our personal lives, and our relationships. All that remains is for us to follow these teachings and live our lives according to what we have seen in God's Word. Our actions must be an expression of what we know and believe. Our goal is to serve God in a way that is acceptable to Him.

Serving God because of Who He Is

In our sharing about the love and the grace of God, we must not overlook who God is. Hebrews 12:28–29 reminds us of God's awesomeness. How is God described here?

____

The background of this Scripture is the giving of the law in Exodus 19:18–25, when the mountain quaked and erupted with fire because of the presence of God. The writer of Hebrews says God will again shake the world, and only the kingdom of God will remain (Hebrews 12:26–28). The exact fulfillment of these verses remains to be seen, but they give us insight into the awesome power of the God we serve.

The manner of our service to Him is also listed in verse 28. What two things are to characterize our service?

____

In acquiring a knowledge of love and grace, we must not lose our sense of awe of the One we serve, the majestic God of the universe who has all power and all knowledge.

Serving God Acceptably because of Jesus

One issue we have not discussed to this point is suffering for Christ's sake. When people are serving God, trying to do right, living in love and peace, it would seem that all would go well for them. But sometimes it does not. Sometimes they suffer persecution simply because they are Christians. What is acceptable service in these cases?

Peter gives us guidelines in his first epistle. Read 1 Peter 2:11–25. Make a brief outline of his instructions to Christians, showing how they are to live.

Verse 11 ______________________________

Verse 12 ______________________________

Verse 13 ______________________________

Verse 17 ______________________________

Verse 18 ______________________________

Even living in this upright way, Christians may sometimes be treated harshly. What are they to do then?

Verses 19–20 ______________________________

Patiently enduring harsh treatment when we have done no wrong is not easy. In fact, it is contrary to our human nature and would be impossible if it were not for the Spirit of God working in our lives. We also have the example of Jesus to follow. Continue the Scripture reading to see how He responded to suffering. What things did He not do?

Verse 23 ______________________________

____

In addition to these things listed that Jesus did *not* do, what is listed that He *did* do?

Verse 23 ______________________________

This patient endurance of unjust suffering is "acceptable," or pleasing, to God, according to verse 20. Peter concludes the passage by encouraging those who are suffering to "commit themselves" to God (1 Peter 4:19). We express our trust in God by enduring hardships patiently. This is well pleasing to Him.

Serving God Acceptably because of His Word

Our studies thus far have taken us to many parts of the Bible. We have seen how God has revealed himself through His Word in different times and different places. Undergirding our studies is a basic belief that God's Word is true. This is the foundation for our faith in Him and our desire to please Him.

The principles we have studied are not just human ideas, which often change with the mere move to another culture or the inevitable passing of time. We have explored principles of God's Word, which will endure forever. God has declared that His Word will stand because He is God. Read Isaiah 46:9–10 where this declaration is made. What does God say He will do?

Verse 10 ____

Not only will God's Word stand forever, but it will also accomplish what He pleases in the earth. Read Isaiah 55:8–11. What illustration does God use to show the effect of His Word?

Verse 10 ____

God has said His Word will not return to Him "empty," "void" (KJV), "fruitless" (NEB), but will accomplish what He pleases. If His Word is so powerful and so effective, we should do all we can to understand His Word and guide our lives by it.

Serving God Acceptably because of Who We Are

Our desire to serve God acceptably is a reflection of who we are. We are no longer our own; we have been bought with a price, the blood of Jesus (1 Corinthians 6:19–20; 1 Peter 1:18–19). We belong to God. We are children of the Kingdom.

When we were in the pastorate and our children were small, we were concerned about their understanding that family rules were *family* rules, not those of the church. We carefully tried to maintain a strong sense of family so that decisions were made on the basis of what the family stood for, not what someone else thought. Situations were discussed so the children understood our thinking, why we preferred they do or not do certain things. Frequently as they would be leaving the house we would remind them, "Remember who you are." Hopefully they would remember that they belonged to parents who loved them and who had a code of behavior based on family rules that made sense. (It worked most of the time.)

It is important to our Christian conduct to remember who we are in God. We are not just ordinary people, living ordinary lives. We must constantly remember that we belong to a Heavenly Father who loves us and cares how we live. This knowledge can affect every aspect of our behavior. For we should live so that we bring honor to His name, reflecting His love for us.

Before our conversion we were natural beings; now we have added the spiritual dimension to our lives. Our spiritual desires should now direct us. In writing to the Romans, Paul encouraged believers to "walk not after the flesh, but after the Spirit" (Romans 8:1, KJV). He adds that "those controlled by the sinful nature cannot please God" (Romans 8:8).

If our desire is to "walk . . . after the Spirit," we will have a conscious desire to please God in the areas we have been studying. We will want our worship, our actions, and our relationships to be pleasing to Him.

For serving God acceptably, the King James Version translates Hebrews 12:28, "Let us have grace." The Greek word for grace, *charis,* is sometimes translated "favor." It is used of Mary (Luke 1:30), Jesus (Luke 2:52), and David (Acts 7:46), all of whom found favor with God. This is the grace that brought us to God in the first place. It enables us to be like Jesus, even if it means suffering because we are trusting in God's Word. Through His grace we are able to please Him.

Accompanying this grace is always a godly fear, or "reverence and awe," as the writer of Hebrews puts it. We never lose the sense of who it is we are trying to serve and please. We remember who He is, the great God of the universe, and who we are, His children who want to please Him.

An appropriate prayer to conclude our studies is the prayer of David in Psalm 19:14:

"May the words of my mouth [all public situations]
and the meditation of my heart [all private thoughts]
be pleasing
in your sight,
O Lord, my Rock and my Redeemer."

Think About It

Contemplate for a few minutes your knowledge of God. Review your list of the characteristics of God from chapter 2. Did you include the characteristic we studied in this chapter, His awesome power that will one day shake the heavens and earth?

How would you explain a God who is loving, gracious, and kind but who is also a God who judges sin?

____

____

____

Review the characteristics of Jesus that you listed in chapter 4. Did you include His patience in suffering as one of the characteristics we should have if we want to be like Him?

Suffering for Christ's sake is a dimension of Christian service we do not often discuss. How can we prepare ourselves if we are called upon to suffer for Christ? List three ways.

____

____

____

With a basic assumption that the Word of God is true and will stand throughout eternity, this entire study has been based upon its teachings. What are the purposes of Scripture according to 2 Timothy 3:15–17?

Are you using the Scriptures in these ways in your life?

Review your summary statement at the conclusion of chapter 6, describing the way in which you choose to please God. Does this statement need to be enlarged or changed in any way? As a conclusion to this study, reaffirm your commitment to please God in every aspect of your life. Confirm that commitment with a written summary statement, showing your determination to please God, for future reference.

Notes